E OF WASHINGTON.

THIS BOOK BELONGS TO

George Washington Notebook
Copyright © 2017 by Appleseed Press Book Publishers LLC.

This is an officially licensed book by Cider Mill Press Book Publishers LLC.

All rights reserved under the Pan-American and International Copyright Conventions.

No part of this book may be reproduced in whole or in part, scanned, photocopied, recorded, distributed in any printed or electronic form, or reproduced in any manner whatsoever, or by any information storage and retrieval system now known or hereafter invented, without express written permission of the publisher, except in the case of brief quotations embodied in critical articles and reviews.

The scanning, uploading, and distribution of this book via the Internet or via any other means without permission of the publisher is illegal and punishable by law. Please support authors' rights, and do not participate in or encourage piracy of copyrighted materials.

13-Digit ISBN: 978-1-60433-720-4
10-Digit ISBN: 1-60433-720-6

This book may be ordered by mail from the publisher. Please include $5.99 for postage and handling. Please support your local bookseller first!

Books published by Cider Mill Press Book Publishers are available at special discounts for bulk purchases in the United States by corporations, institutions, and other organizations. For more information, please contact the publisher.

Cider Mill Press Book Publishers
Where good books are ready for press
PO Box 454
12 Spring Street
Kennebunkport, Maine 04046

Visit us on the Web!
www.cidermillpress.com

Cover design by Annalisa Sheldahl
Interior design by Alicia Freile, Tango Media
Typography: Didot, Georgia, and Voluta Script Pro

Image credits in order of appearance:
Cover wrap image: George Washington (Shutterstock); George Washington's signature (Wikimedia Commons); front endpapers: George Washington's home at Mount Vernon, Virginia (Shutterstock), and George Washington (Shutterstock); George Washington to Matthias Ogden, Draft, August 31, 1778 (Library of Congress, George Washington Papers collection, Manuscript Division); General George Washington (Shutterstock); The Battle of Yorktown (Shutterstock); General George Washington Taking Leave of the Officers of his Army (Shutterstock); Mount Rushmore—George Washington Sculpture (Shutterstock); George Washington (Library of Congress, Prints and Photographs Division LC-DIG-pga-00217); George Washington's Second Inauguration (Shutterstock); U.S. President George Washington, being inaugurated in New York City (Shutterstock); George Washington Statue in Boston Public Garden (Shutterstock); George Washington painted by Gilbert Stuart (Library of Congress, Prints and Photographs LC-USZ62-7585); General George Washington (center), depicted in the Surrender of Cornwallis in Yorktown, 1781 (Shutterstock); George Washington and his grandchildren (Shutterstock); George Washington and the Cherry Tree (Shutterstock); Drawing of Etienne De Lancey house, published in *Appleton's Cyclopaedia of American Biography*, 1900 (Wikimedia); back endpapers: Burial tomb of George Washington at Mount Vernon in Virginia (Shutterstock); Washington Monument (Shutterstock).

Printed in China
1 2 3 4 5 6 7 8 9 0
First Edition

GEORGE WASHINGTON

NOTEBOOK

KENNEBUNKPORT, MAINE

Introduction

By John Burns, author of *The Call of Patriotism*

Nearly every American knows the story of George Washington. Born to a wealthy landowning Virginia family, he volunteered for the British colonial militia. He distinguished himself in the French and Indian War for his bravery, courage, and leadership skills. After gaining notoriety during the war, Washington retired to his family estate at Mount Vernon. He married Martha Custis and devoted himself to the plantation's affairs. During the 1760s, Washington was a vocal opponent of the Crown's taxation policies in the Colonies. In several letters to other Revolutionary leaders, Washington decried the colonial system that gave the British Monarch tyrannical authority over the Colonies' individual economic affairs.

On the eve of the American Revolution, as the Continental Congress gathered, it was Washington who they tapped to lead the Continental Army. One must presume this decision was not based solely on his military attributes but his devotion to the cause of democracy. During the Revolution, he represented the ethos of American democracy: self-government, individual leadership, and a dedication to liberty. General Washington distinguished himself as both a strong military leader and a powerful representation of the values of the new nation.

But once the war was over, Washington's mission was far from complete. Although the great task of defeating the British required immense patience, careful planning, and much sacrifice, it wasn't Washington's biggest challenge. When he was elected President and took office, he had no historical precedence, no guide for how to run the office of the President of the United States.

He relied upon his love of his country and his love of freedom to lead him through these unchartered waters. During his presidency, he dealt with domestic uprisings, war debt, and international relationships.

When his second term neared its conclusion and he prepared to relinquish his duties as President, many feared the tyrannical regimes of centuries past. American democracy had yet to face one of its greatest challenges: the peaceful transition of power. The Constitution prescribed free and fair elections and the process for electing a different president. But, there was no certainty that President Washington would give up his position. Although the Constitution *created* the Presidency, Washington *made* the Presidency. And he peacefully left his post and returned to Mount Vernon for the remainder of his life.

Take a trip to Mount Vernon and you'll gain an appreciation of George Washington's brilliance. The grounds and mansion are spectacular. From the gardens to the fields, from the salt house to the kitchen, every part of the first First Family's estate is a wonder. As you walk through the house and walk the literal footsteps of so many prominent members of our nation's early history, you begin to appreciate the power of a man like George Washington.

The Washingtons loved to entertain and many legendary people visited Mount Vernon to pay their respects to the American first "First" Family. Indeed, one of Washington's most admirable traits was his desire to spent his days with his friends rather than in the presence of celebrities and global icons.

When George Washington took office in 1789, he had only a Congress and a Constitution. He was a leader that brought Americans together and healed divisions. Washington represents that which we expect in our leaders today. He had strong personal convictions and stayed true to his principles and values. He was a leader that listened. As our only independent president, he was also a leader that respected other viewpoints. His intellectual prowess was unmatched and will keep his place in the annals of history as one of the world's greatest political leaders.

Today he is remembered as the great commander of the Revolutionary War and the father of our country, and for good reason. He possessed the gravitas and charismatic tendencies we've come to expect of all our Commanders-in-Chief since him.

George Washington to Matthias Ogden, Draft (August 31, 1778)

McHenry

Head Quarters
Orville
31st Aug't 1778

Sir

I would wish in case you
a can put in
have caused [an] execution the plan
for the obtaining intelligence that you
would to imploy it on the following
objects. They are of much importance
to be known and the facts should be
established as soon as possible.
and the particular corps
— What number of troops, embarked
on board the transports that went up
the sound & how many in the vessels
that sailed from the Hook — without
the stock
with what artillery and provision
— whether provided the sufficiency the latter
for a long or short voyage — What
general Officers commanded.
Whether Gen. Clinton — or Cornwallis
or both —
every
I wish to have these facts
established as soon as possible and
by ...... when ...... known.
...... by ...... I am &c
Col. Ogden

Observe good faith and justice towards all Nations;
CULTIVATE PEACE AND HARMONY WITH ALL.

—Farewell Address (September 19, 1796)

To be prepared for war is one of the most effectual means of **PRESERVING PEACE.**

—First Annual Address to Both Houses of Congress (January 8, 1790)

General George Washington

THE FREEDOM OF SPEECH MAY BE TAKEN AWAY,

and, dumb and silent we may be led, like sheep, to the Slaughter.

—Address to the officers of the army (March 15, 1783)

The Battle of Yorktown

> Our cause is noble
> # IT IS THE CAUSE OF MANKIND!
>
> —Letter to James Warren
> (March 31, 1779)

We should never despair, our Situation before has been unpromising and

HAS CHANGED FOR THE BETTER,

so I trust, it will again.

—Letter to Major General Philip Schuyler regarding the fall of Fort Ticonderoga (July 15, 1777)

THE NAME OF AMERICAN,

which belongs to you, in your national capacity, must always exalt

THE JUST PRIDE OF PATRIOTISM,

more than any appellation derived from local discriminations.

—Farewell Address (September 19, 1796)

General George Washington taking leave of the officers of his army

While we are contending for our own liberty, **WE SHOULD BE VERY CAUTIOUS NOT TO VIOLATE THE RIGHTS OF CONSCIENCE IN OTHERS...**

—Letter to Benedict Arnold (September 14, 1775)

Mount Rushmore—George Washington sculpture

I hold the maxim no less applicable to public than to private affairs, that

HONESTY IS THE BEST POLICY.

—Farewell Address (September 19, 1796)

I most devoutly wish that your latter days may be as prosperous and happy, as your former ones have been **GLORIOUS AND HONOURABLE.**

—Farewell message to officers at Fraunces Tavern, New York City (December 4, 1783)

Do not conceive that fine Clothes make fine Men,

ANY MORE THAN FINE FEATHERS MAKE FINE BIRDS.

—Letter to nephew Bushrod Washington (January 15, 1783)

George Washington

George Washington's Second Inauguration

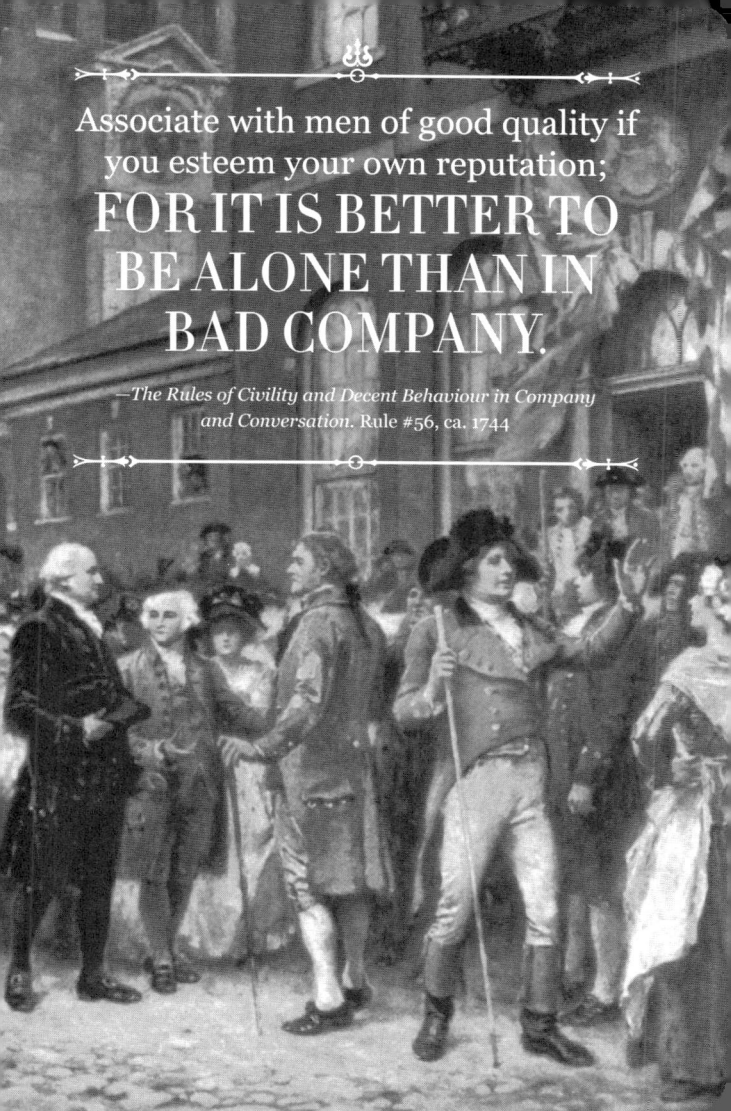

Associate with men of good quality if you esteem your own reputation; FOR IT IS BETTER TO BE ALONE THAN IN BAD COMPANY.

—*The Rules of Civility and Decent Behaviour in Company and Conversation.* Rule #56, ca. 1744

BE COURTEOUS TO ALL, BUT INTIMATE WITH FEW,

and let those few be well tried before you give them your confidence...

—Letter to nephew Bushrod Washington (January 15, 1783)

President George Washington being inaugurated in New York City

...a good moral character is the first essential in a man... It is therefore highly important that

YOU SHOULD ENDEAVOR NOT ONLY TO BE LEARNED BUT VIRTUOUS.

—Letter to nephew Steptoe Washington (December 5, 1790)

...HAPPINESS AND MORAL DUTY

are inseparably connected...

—Message to the Protestant Episcopal Church (August 19, 1789)

George Washington statue in Boston Public Garden

THE BASIS OF OUR POLITICAL SYSTEMS, IS THE RIGHT OF THE PEOPLE TO MAKE AND TO ALTER THEIR CONSTITUTIONS OF GOVERNMENT.

—Farewell Address (September 19, 1796)

George Washington

Speak seldom, but to important subjects...

—Letter to nephew Bushrod Washington (November 10, 1787)

General George Washington (center), depicted at the surrender of Cornwallis in Yorktown, 1781

We must take
human nature as we find it,
PERFECTION FALLS NOT TO THE SHARE OF MORTALS.

—Letter to John Jay (August 15, 1786)

Knowledge is in every Country

THE SUREST BASIS OF PUBLIC HAPPINESS.

— First Annual Address to Both Houses of Congress
(January 8, 1790)

We are either
A UNITED PEOPLE,
or we are not. If the former,
let us, in all maters
of general concern
ACT AS A NATION...

—Letter to James Madison (November 30, 1785)

George Washington with his grandchildren

Guard against the impostures of

PRETEND PATRIOTISM.

—Farewell Address (September 19, 1796)

George Washington and the cherry tree

Still I hope I shall always possess firmness and virtue enough to maintain

(WHAT I CONSIDER THE MOST ENVIABLE OF ALL TITLES)

the character of an honest man.

—Letter to Alexander Hamilton (August 28, 1788)

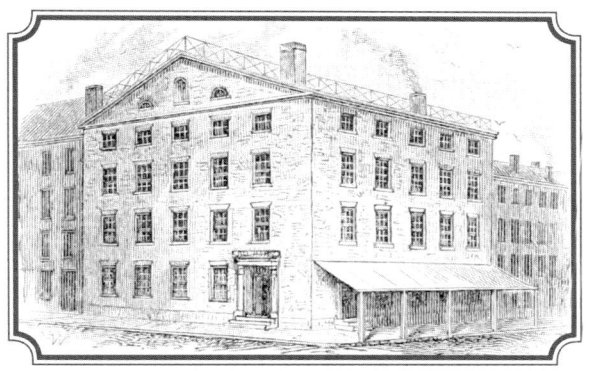

Etienne De Lancey House, the forerunner of Fraunces Tavern in New York, where Washington bade farewell to his army

About Cider Mill Press Book Publishers

Good ideas ripen with time. From seed to harvest, Cider Mill Press brings fine reading, information, and entertainment together between the covers of its creatively crafted books. Our Cider Mill bears fruit twice a year, publishing a new crop of titles each spring and fall.

Visit us on the web at
www.cidermillpress.com
or write to us at
12 Spring Street
PO Box 454
Kennebunkport, Maine 04046